Your Brand, Your Voice

How Communication Shapes Your Personal Brand

Table of Contents

Chapter 1. Introduction

Welcome to a universe of unearthing your true potential through our Special Report, "Your Brand, Your Voice: How Communication Shapes Your Personal Brand." In a world swarming with sameness, let's take an explorative path towards amplifying uniqueness. This compelling report delves deep into the science of self-expression, explicating how adept communication is far more than simply transferring thoughts but a powerful tool for personal brand shaping. From narrative crafting to handling criticism, the report uncovers the secrets behind the most successful personal brands, establishing your voice as your ultimate branding cohort. You're just one click away from a transformative journey into personal branding. Now, don't just be another face in the crowd. Buy this special report to illuminate your distinctiveness and make an unforgettable mark in your respective field with an undeniably authentic, influential voice!

Chapter 2. Unwrapping Your Personal Brand

The journey towards acquiring a personal brand that resonates with your audience begins with a rigorous self-assessment. You must probe beneath the layers of your personality, your preferences, and your aspirations.

2.1. Identifying Your Personal Attributes

Start by questioning what makes you, you. Think about your strengths, your passions, and your unique attributes. These elements represent the raw material for building your personal brand. Consider what distinguishes you from others. Is it your delectable sense of humor, your knack for storytelling, your authenticity, or your ability to inspire others?

Next, determine your core values and principles. What are the constants in your life that you've regularly upheld? Core values can include things like hard work, authenticity, creativity, or compassion. Your principles act as your personal compass, guiding you towards consistency, which is a paramount attribute of a strong personal brand.

2.2. Leveraging Your Unique Selling Proposition

Every brand needs a unique selling proposition (USP) that sets it apart from its competitors. As the term suggests, your USP should be something uniquely yours. This could be a specific skill, a particular experience, a unique perspective, or some blend of these. For example, your USP could be your unparalleled expertise in project management, your intuitive knack for forecasting market trends, or your unique brand of motivational speaking. Define this clearly, as your USP should trickle down to every piece of content, interaction, or communication associated with your brand.

2.3. Match Your Image to Your Brand

We live in a visually driven society, and the personal brand you project should closely align with your visual image. Whether it's your personal style, your online presence, or your physical office space, all need to convey a consistent message about your brand. Cultivating a strong visual brand that resonates with your target audience is critical. A well-thought-out visual identity can significantly enhance your personal brand recognition and elicit an emotional connection with your audience.

2.4. Building a Narrative Around Your Brand

A defining element of your personal brand is the narrative that surrounds it. People resonate with stories. Be the author of your own story, developing a narrative that supports your personal brand and exemplifies your unique attributes, values, and USP. This narrative can incorporate your journey, your struggles, your successes, and your future aspirations.

2.5. Manifest Your Brand through Your Communications

The language, the style, the tone of voice you use in your

communications all play a significant role in shaping your personal brand. Whether it's through your written or spoken words, be conscious of how you express yourself. Your communication style should consistently echo your personal brand, reinforcing your unique attributes and values.

2.6. Building and Managing Your Online Presence

In a world interconnected through digital channels, your online presence forms a key aspect of your personal brand. Managing your digital identity involves curating content, engaging with your audience, and effectively using SEO to increase your visibility. Regularly update your online presence to align with your personal brand's evolution.

2.7. Handling Criticism and Challenges

Becoming a personal brand involves being in the spotlight, which invariably welcomes both praise and criticism. Handling the latter constructively is a key skill that builds your brand's resilience. Also, remember to face challenges head-on, showcasing your grit and determination. These experiences can even form a compelling segment of your brand narrative.

2.8. Flexibility in Brand Development

While consistency is crucial, so is adaptability. The dynamic nature of both professional and personal landscapes necessitates a brand that can evolve without losing its core essence. Embrace changes as opportunities for growth and incorporate them as positive elements into your brand development process.

Unfolding your personal brand isn't a one-step process. It's treading a path of introspection and transparency, evoking trustworthiness while also embodying consistency. It's about asserting your uniqueness in a sea of sameness. Above all, a successful personal brand lies in authenticity, in being true to your inner self. Embrace your individuality, and let it shape a unique branding experience that resonates with your audience - that's the charm of unravelling your personal brand.

Chapter 3. Your Communication: A Mirror to Your Brand

In the vast landscape of contemporary branding, communication forms an integral reflection of your personal brand. Widely referred to as the mirroring effect, it implies that how you communicate is an essential part of how people perceive your brand. Whether you're a seasoned business professional, a blooming entrepreneur, or an aspiring influencer, understanding this powerful coupling of communication and personal branding is key to emerging from the crowd.

3.1. The Mirroring Effect

Unbeknownst to many, everything we say - and the way we choose to say it - contributes to the image we project. This notion is not trivial; it has been supported by numerous studies in social psychology and communication. This phenomenon, also known as the mirroring effect, encompasses both verbal and non-verbal cues: words, inflection, pauses, facial expressions, and body language.

This phenomenon is not passive. Proactive monitoring and management of this mirror create a consistent and compelling brand image. Gauge what your communication style reflects about you. Does it exude confidence, showcase innovation, or project empathy? Understand what your brand stands for and align your communication to reflect these values.

3.2. Curating Your Verbal Communication

Verbal communication embodies everything from the words you use to the anecdotes you choose. A few strategies for maximizing the impact of your verbal communication include:

1. Clarity: Use language that is precise, concise, and easy to understand.

2. Storytelling: Craft a narrative that compels your audience and strengthens the relatability of your brand.

3. Consistency: Be consistent in the themes and values echoed through your stories, ensuring they reflect your brand's identity.

4. Emotion: Convey genuine emotion to foster a sense of shared experience with your audience.

3.3. Synchronizing Non-Verbal Communication

Non-verbal cues play an equally significant role in rounding off your brand's image. From posture to facial expressions, the subtleties of non-verbal communication can drastically influence perceptions. If your words say one thing while your body signals another, audiences can feel disconnected. Consistency and coherence between your verbal message and non-verbal cues are crucial for creating an authentic brand image.

3.4. Criticism: A Bridge, Not a Barrier

Criticism is an inevitable part of the communication and branding journey. Rather than approaching criticism defensively, viewing it as a learning opportunity can fortify your personal brand. How you respond to criticism communicates as much about your brand and its values as your original message. Practicing resilience and openness to improvement makes for a brand that is not only mature but also relatable and human.

3.5. Cultivating Adaptability: Different Strokes for Different Folks

While a consistent message is critical, adaptability is a valuable skill. Different situations or audiences may necessitate slight adjustments in your communication style. Anticipating and understanding these nuances allows you to adjust tactically without diluting your brand's core values.

3.6. The Weight of Digital Communication

With the rise of digital platforms, the way we communicate our personal brand has expanded and evolved. Our digital footprint—social media posts, emails, blog posts—provides another reflective surface for our brand. Considering digital environments in your communication plan generates a more complete and current image.

3.7. Walking the Talk: The Power of Action

Actions genuinely speak louder than words. What you do, how you react, and how you interact with others are all observed and absorbed by your audience, further shaping their perception.

Ensuring your actions align with your verbal and non-verbal communication builds a potent brand image, solidifying the adage that branding is all about walking the talk.

As this exploration into the role of communication in personal branding unveils, the essence lies in knowing who you are, being consistent, and welcoming growth. Your communication reflects your brand, so shine the best light on it, and remember, every interaction provides an opportunity to showcase the unique brand that is you.

Chapter 4. Art of Crafting a Compelling Narrative

An insight-provoking narrative is more than just spinning a story; it's about formulating an authentic, compelling tale that truly represents your brand identity. In the process, it helps differentiate your brand, shape perceptions, and forge a meaningful connection with the audience. Thus, meticulously crafting your narrative is integral in personal branding.

4.1. Understanding the Core Elements of a Compelling Narrative

Every story has three core elements: characters, plot, and resolution. In the context of personal branding, the 'character' refers to you, the 'plot' is your journey, and the 'resolution' refers to how you resolved challenges along the way.

An engaging narrative makes use of a unique combination of details about your life, values, talents, and purpose. Adding such elements of human interest to a narrative makes it relatable for the audience. Your unique journey and the principles you've upheld throughout can chart a fascinating story of resilience, innovation, or any theme that reverberates with your brand.

4.2. Drawing from Personal Experience

A compelling narrative must involve your personal experiences. Reflect on your life journey, derive insights from all your moments—successes, failures, turning points—and encode these insights into your narrative. Remember, your experiences are unique to you; they can't be replicated. This uniqueness is a vital ingredient in creating an exclusive brand narrative.

Likewise, your values speak volumes about your brand's essence. From serving as your compass in decision-making to shaping your interactions, they greatly determine your actions. Intertwining these deeply-held beliefs into your narrative allows your audience to comprehend what drives you, giving them a meaningful impression of your brand.

4.3. Unearthing Your Unique Selling Proposition (USP)

Your USP is an intrinsic component of your personal brand narrative. It's that distinguishing factor that separates you from the rest. Your USP could be anything from a remarkable skill, a unique approach, an impressive accomplishment, or your innovative vision. Defining this helps underscore what your value addition would be, setting up an expectation for what your audience can consistently anticipate from you.

4.4. Constructing the Narrative Arc

A narrative arc invigorates your story with a structure—beginning, middle, and end. It helps chart your journey in a cohesive, linear manner, drawing the audience in and maintaining their interest throughout your story.

The beginning introduces you and sets the stage for your story. The middle explores the challenges you've faced, the choices you made, and the changes you experienced. Lastly, the end or climax resolves the conflicts and realizations from your journey, serving as an exposition of your current brand persona.

4.5. Choice of Language and Tone

The language and tone employed speak volumes about your brand's persona. Whether you adopt formal language, approachable vernacular, polished grammar, or a blend of these, your choice highly influences how your brand is perceived. A consistent tone aids in leaving a memorable imprint of your brand in the minds of your audience.

4.6. Reiterating Your Brand's Vision

Your vision symbolizes your brand's direction. Where do you see yourself in the future? What are your ambitions? Inculcating your vision into your narrative provides an exciting glimpse to your audience about your brand's future, inspiring them to become a part of your journey.

In conclusion, crafting a compelling narrative provides an opportunity for your audience to experience and understand the journey behind your personal brand. It's the umbilical cord that connects your present to your past and projects your future. It resonates with your persona, reputation, and value proposition, ultimately serving as a beacon that highlights your distinctiveness in a crowded marketplace. By harnessing these tips into practice, you truly can say: "That's my story, and I'm sticking to it!"

Chapter 5. Polishing Your Personal Brand: The Role of Feedback

Intensified competition in today's professional market demands that individuals shape and refine their personal brand constantly. A key instrument facilitating this process is feedback; both receiving and constructively utilizing it to improve one's brand can significantly impact your personal brand's perception and effectiveness.

5.1. Understanding the Importance of Feedback

Feedback, as simple as it may sound, is a two-fold mechanism comprising giving and receiving information about an individual's performance relative to certain standards. Whether positive or negative, it opens up new possibilities to learn, grow, and polish your personal brand. It provides an outsider's perspective, revealing blind spots, and challenging our inherent assumptions, thus cultivating a clearer, more precise vision of one's own brand.

5.2. Attaining Feedback: The Right Approach

Zig Ziglar once said, "The only thing worse than training employees and losing them is not training them, and keeping them." This also holds true for individual personal brand development. There's an immense need to identify the right people and sources to attain feedback from in order to nurture your brand's growth. Colleagues, mentors, superiors, or even clients, everyone holds a unique perspective. At the heart of constructive feedback lies an honest, diplomatic expression that is born out of observance and shared with the intent to bring about positive change.

5.3. Constructive Criticism: A Brand-Polishing Tool

Undeniably, constructive criticism is the cornerstone of effective feedback. While most view criticism negatively, adopting an open mindset towards it can aid in the emergence of strong personal brands. Constructive criticism exposes weaknesses, thus delivering a reality-check to aid you in rectifying errors and filling gaps. This, in turn, helps stand out.

5.4. The Feedback Loop: Utilizing Positive Feedback

Positive feedback tends to act as a booster for morale and efficiency. It reinforces the right behaviors and actions, further encouraging you to continue working on those aspects. While useful, the objective here is to not just rest on laurels but rather use this positive feedback to identify your strengths, and then leverage them to amplify your personal brand.

5.5. Handling Negative Feedback: Refining the Rough Edges

The prospect of receiving negative feedback can be intimidating. However, a mindset shift can turn this into a constructively altering experience. Recognizing negative feedback as an opportunity for refinement is key to utilize it in polishing your personal brand. This lies in managing one's emotional responses towards criticism, actively listening for areas of improvement, and implementing the change.

5.6. Living the Change: Implementing Feedback

The entire process of attaining and analyzing feedback falls flat if the final step of its execution doesn't witness light. Actions speak louder than words. To ensure that the garnered feedback doesn't go wasted, one must make an action plan and stick to it. Regular evaluations of your progress and acknowledging the changes you've undergone can further help solidify modifications in your personal brand.

5.7. Taking it Forward: Creating a Feedback Culture

In a world where everybody has a voice, creating a feedback culture can assist in iterative polishing of personal brands. Regularly asking for feedback signals that you're receptive and committed to bettering yourself, thereby propelling others to become more vocal too. This not only promotes healthy communication but also generates a cycle of continual improvement, beneficial for all involved.

Through sculpting our inferences and enhancing our actions, feedback acts as a sharpening apparatus for your personal brand. It's a never-ending journey rather than a particular destination. Feedback is not about perfecting something on one go but improving bit by bit, relentlessly. Therefore, embrace this powerful tool to let your brand shine the brightest.

Chapter 6. Noise to Signal: Distilling Your Message in a Cluttered World

In a world teeming with information, the ability to streamline your message and rise above the rest is invaluable. The ever-growing anthem of information, often referred to as 'Noise,' can drown out your voice and sabotage your personal brand if not adequately managed. Therefore, it's vital that we understand how to transform the 'Noise' into 'Signal', using it not as a hindrance, but a tool to accentuate our uniqueness and effectively pass our messages across.

6.1. Understanding Noise and Signal in Communication

In communication theory, 'Noise' represents unwanted or distractive information that can mar the effectiveness of your message. 'Signal', on the other hand, is the meaningful, desired information. In the context of personal branding, the 'Noise' is any piece of meddling information that disrupts your message from being heard, comprehended, and retained by your audience. The 'Signal' is your clear, distinct message, which reflects your personal brand.

In today's digital age, 'Noise' can take countless forms - from countless emails flooding inboxes, social media feeds overrun with content, to web pages rampant with aggressive advertising. Everyone is shouting to be heard, creating a cacophony of messages.

The goal is to transform 'Noise' into an unambiguous 'Signal.' Ensuring that your message stands out, it is taken in and remembered for all the right reasons.

6.2. The Importance of Clear Communication in Personal Branding

Your personal brand is essentially a unique blend of your skills, experiences, and personality traits that you express to the world. Each interaction you have, every post you make on social media is a brush stroke in the painting that is your public persona. Communicating your personal brand effectively and clearly can make the difference between being lost in the sea of 'Noise' or standing out as a respected and influential voice in your field.

To ensure that your message is received as intended, it is crucial that your communication is clarity personified. Clear communication reduces misunderstanding, promotes trust, and can save precious time and resources.

6.3. Techniques to Refine Your Message

Developing, executing, and maintaining an effective communication strategy are paramount to mitigate the noise. Below are some key steps to consider:

1. Identify your Message: First and foremost, you need to understand what message you wish to communicate. What are the core values and elements of your personal brand that you want to be known for? Once you have a clear idea of this, you can begin to shape your communication around it.

2. Know Your Audience: It's vital to understand not only who your audience is but also their preferences, needs, and the platforms they frequent.

3. Stay Consistent: Consistency is king when it comes to branding. When your message is consistent, it's easier for people to remember and to understand what you stand for.

4. Use Visuals: Visual content can help cut through the digital noise. Infographics, images, and videos can grab attention and help effectively communicate your message.

5. Keep it Simple: Avoid jargon and complexity. Use clear, concise language that your audience can quickly understand.

6. Emotional Connections: Communicate with empathy and emotional intelligence. Help your audience feel connected to your message.

6.4. Riding the Waves of Digital Noise

Amidst the digital noise, it's about creating a signal that not only stands out but also resonates with your audience. It's about crafting your message in a way that makes people pay attention, understand, remember, and act upon it. Ultimately, the power of your 'Signal' in the noisy world rests in your hands.

By understanding the intricacies of 'Noise' and 'Signal' in communication and applying the principles of clear communication and message refinement, you can navigate through the cluttered world of information, ensure that your voice is heard, and your personal brand shines.

With practice and patience, you will be able to consistently turn 'Noise' into 'Signal' - applying this powerful understanding to shape your communication strategy and propel your personal brand forward, one confident message at a time.

Chapter 7. The Power of Emotional Intelligence in Personal Branding

Understanding one's own emotions as well as those of others, interpreting them, and applying this knowledge in practical scenarios forms the core of emotional intelligence. In essence, rooting emotional intelligence within your personal brand can be a game-changer for both your professional and personal life. These abilities help with managing relationships, navigating social networks, influencing and inspiring others, and achieving your aspirations.

7.1. Emotional Intelligence: A Deep Dive

As we seek to comprehend the genuine influence of emotional intelligence on a personal brand, we first have to dig into what it truly represents. Emotional intelligence, as popularized by psychologist Daniel Goleman, encompasses five pivotal components: self-awareness, self-regulation, motivation, empathy, and social skills. All these elements, rolled together, work as the backbone for creating an authentic, affable, and influential personal brand.

Self-awareness is the cornerstone of understanding your emotions and their influence on your actions. Those with high self-awareness can identify their strengths and weaknesses, drive themselves towards growth, and provide a genuine reflection of themselves to others.

Moving to self-regulation, it emphasizes managing your emotions healthily and expressing them appropriately. People with good self-regulation do not make impulsive decisions, are open to change, and can effectively handle difficult situations.

Motivation, another critical component, includes striving for goals with resilience and energy, even in the face of setbacks. Those who are self-motivated are highly productive and embrace opportunities for change.

This brings us to empathy - the ability to comprehend and share the feelings of others. Individuals who can empathize can form strong, mutually beneficial relationships, understand different perspectives, and respect others' needs.

Finally, social skills guide us in managing relationships and building networks. It is about how you interact with others - your ability to communicate, guide, and influence people, manage conflicts, and inspire a positive work environment.

7.2. Emotional Intelligence and Your Personal Brand

The key to successful personal branding is authenticity. Your personal brand is your commitment to your persona, a promise of consistency and trustworthiness. A significant aspect of that authenticity is derived from your emotional intelligence.

Self-aware individuals who understand their own emotions and how they are perceived by others can create a brand that truly reflects who they are. Self-regulation ensures the brand stays consistent and reliable, even during times of high stress or conflict. Motivation drives continuous improvement, pushing the brand to new heights.

High levels of empathy mean that not only are you attuned to your feelings, but you can also enter into someone else's feeling state. This makes you outstanding in customer relations and in any other professional or personal role that calls for interaction with people. Effective social skills round out the picture, ensuring that your brand is viewed favorably by those you interact with, and that people will want to keep interacting with your brand.

7.3. Developing Emotional Intelligence into Your Personal Brand

To create an authentic personal brand, the first step is to gain a clear understanding of your current level of emotional intelligence. Take an emotional intelligence assessment, ideally one that provides detailed feedback. Use this as a starting point to understand the areas where you need to focus growth.

Once you have this understanding, start focusing on developing individual components of emotional intelligence in your daily life. Make it a point to be aware of your emotions and understand their impact on your decisions. Practice self-regulation by staying calm in stressful situations, reflecting before reacting, and thinking ahead of time about potential emotional triggers. Develop your empathy by actively trying to see situations from others' perspectives.

Practicing and developing your emotional intelligence requires ongoing commitment. A dedicated effort to regularly engaging in these behaviors can help embed them in your personal brand. Over time, this shift towards emotional intelligence will help shape your persona into a trustworthy, approachable, and authentic brand, one that people will be attracted to and respect.

7.4. Leveraging Emotional Intelligence for Brand Success

To fully leverage emotional intelligence, link it directly to your personal brand's mission and vision. Showcase your emotional intelligence in your communications and interactions. Share stories on your social media platforms that reflect your empathy and motivation. Highlight testimonials or feedback from others that speak to your strong interpersonal skills or self-regulation in the face of adversity.

Use emotional intelligence as a unique selling point - make it something that distinguishes you from competitors in your field. When emotional intelligence forms a core part of your personal brand, you'll find you attract more positive interactions, more respect, and more success in your field.

In conclusion, the power of emotional intelligence cannot be overstated as an essential aspect of your personal brand. By understanding your emotions, regulating your responses, and empathizing with others, you can create and maintain an authentic and resonating brand. Emotional intelligence serves as fuel for your personal brand, driving you towards growth and helping you shape an image that stands out in the crowd.

Chapter 8. Fostering Public Speaking: A Gateway to Influence

In the realm of communication, public speaking stands as one of the most direct and impactful methods to convey your personal brand. Possessing the knack to articulate your thoughts lucidly in front of an audience can augment your image exponentially, cementing your reputation as an influencer in your respective sphere.

8.1. Becoming an Assertive Speaker

One of the cornerstones of effective public speaking is assertiveness. An assertive speaker commands attention and respect, effortlessly leading the audience through the narrative. Assertiveness, however, doesn't equate to aggression. It's about expressing your thoughts and ideas respectfully without undermining others' rights.

To cultivate assertiveness, focus on clear, concise communication. Use unambiguous language, simplify complex ideas, and reinforce key points. Make eye contact to engage your listeners and use non-verbal cues like body language to supplement your words, bolstering intensity and indicating confidence.

Your tone of voice matters significantly as well. Strive for calm, composed speech, avoiding monotonous, hurried, or hushed tones. Variations in pitch and emphasis can generate interest and keep your audience engaged.

8.2. Harnessing the Power of Storytelling

Stories have always been a profound way to connect with audiences. A well-told narrative can transport listeners, evoke emotions, and drive home your core message more convincingly than mere facts and data ever could.

To weave an effective story, know your audience. Understand their perspective, identify common ground, and tailor your narrative to resonate with their experiences and beliefs. Ensure your tale has a discernable beginning, middle, and end as this structure remains familiar and easy to follow for most people.

Remember, your story needs to serve your message, and not the other way around. Use powerful imagery and evocative language, but don't let these elements detract from the main point.

8.3. Navigating Through Fear and Anxiety

Fear and anxiety are often the towering walls that deter individuals from public speaking. However, these feelings are more common than you may think, and even the most seasoned speakers experience them. The key is not to eliminate these feelings but to learn how to manage them.

Understand that some anxiety is beneficial. It enhances alertness and fuels the energy required to perform. Turn your focus towards preparation and practice. These are the twin tools that can significantly reduce anxiety.

When you're well-prepared, you'll have a clear course to steer your presentation along. Rehearsing reduces the uncertainty factor, eases delivery, and builds your confidence.

Resort to relaxation techniques like deep breathing and visualization to handle stage fright. Visualize success, not failure. Remember, the audience is there to learn from you, not judge you.

8.4. Proactive Listening and Engagement

Effective public speaking isn't a monologue. It's a dialogue, a two-way flow of communication. Proactive listening can heighten your involvement with the audience, facilitating a conversation rather than a lecture, thus enriching their experience.

Pay attention to audience feedback, both verbal and non-verbal. Encourage questions and be responsive. The more you engage with your audience, the more lively and interactive your speech becomes.

Reflect on questions or statements from your audience without shooting down instant responses. This shows respect for their input and buys you time to frame coherent, well-thought-out responses.

8.5. Conquering Criticism with Grace

Criticism is an indispensable part of public speaking. However, how you manage criticism significantly impacts your personal brand. The first step is to alter your perception of criticism.

View it as a valuable tool for growth instead of an affront. Recognize that all criticism isn't negative, and even negative criticism can yield positive outcomes when you learn from it.

Responding to criticism professionally is pivotal. Maintain an open mind, ask for specifics to avoid misunderstandings, and acknowledge any missteps. See criticism as an opportunity for self-enhancement, propelling you towards becoming a more refined, impactful speaker.

Remember, mastering public speaking is a journey. With time, persistence, and practice, you'll learn to authentically articulate your personal brand, amplify your influence, and ensure your voice resounds powerfully within your sphere.

Chapter 9. Daring to Differ: Building a Unique Brand Persona

In an age dictated by generic templates and stereotypical moulds, the art of standing out has become increasingly complex. However, it's crucial to understand that your brand persona thrives on its uniqueness. To differentiate is to establish your brand persona with a distinct, original voice that oozes authenticity and credibility, taking you miles ahead in the vast context of your domain.

9.1. Understanding the Concept of Unique Brand Persona

Diversity is what makes the world a vibrant place. And it is precisely this diversity that breathes life into your brand persona. With an exclusive approach that boldly reflects your principles, insights, and learned experiences, forming your own unique brand persona isn't an exercise in self-identification, but in perception management. It's about how you project yourself to your audience, and how effectively you convey your distinct traits to the public, inviting engagement, recognition, and appreciation.

To say, every personal brand must own its persona - a character that translates the brand's ethos, objectives, values, and style. Like a stalwart lighthouse beaconing light to the lost voyagers, your brand's persona should guide your audience, resonating your values with them, connecting the dots, and weaving meaningful relations. An outrageous brand persona, unless strikingly relevant, can miserably fail, leaving your audience puzzled and distanced. For this reason, building your unique brand persona requires well-calibrated intelligence, creativity, and authenticity.

9.2. Factors Influencing Unique Brand Persona

While creating a unique brand persona might sound like an art, it is also prompted by a handful of choices and inherited traits. Several factors influence your brand persona:

1. Your voice: The way you communicate significantly impacts how your audience perceives your brand. The language you use, the tone you set, the emotions you convey all harmonize to compose your unique communicative voice.

2. Your values: Your principles and philosophies are the bedrock of your brand identity. They direct your business strategies and decisions, influencing your brand persona.

3. Your target audience: The demographic and psychographic aspects of your audience can determine your brand persona as you will mold your brand persona to connect more seamlessly with them.

4. Your domain or industry: Your niche industry's unique needs, requirements, and issues can shape your persona, its voice, understanding, and approach to the related problems.

9.3. Crafting Your Unique Brand Persona

A magnetic brand persona is an invaluable asset promising rewarding returns. But knowing the elements to focus on while developing this persona may seem like an onerous task. Here are steps you can take in your journey:

1. Identify your attributes: Reflect on what makes you different. You have to delve into everything inclusive of personality traits, linguistic style, background, experiences, and so forth. Draw a comprehensive list of all the attributes potential in shaping your unique brand persona.

2. Understand your audience: Empathize with your audience. Who are they? What are their needs, pain points? What gets their attention? The more in-depth your understanding, the better positioned you will be in delivering a persona that resonates with them.

3. Assemble Your Brand Persona: Fuse your unique attributes with your audience's needs and expectation, contouring your brand persona effortlessly. It will be your beacon, your alter ego, your representative in the public sphere.

9.4. Testing Your Unique Brand Persona

Putting your newly carved brand persona to test is advisable before launching it publicly. Here's how you can do it:

1. Gauge the reaction: Use polls, focus groups, or one-on-one discussions with your targeted audience. It's vital to understand if your persona resonates with them, if it builds that connection you aimed for.

2. Refine based on feedback: Nobody gets it right the first time. Using the feedback you received, iterate on your persona. Refine it until it perfectly aligns with your vision and is well received by the audience.

Creating a brand persona is a marathon, not a sprint. It's an ongoing process that evolves with you and your audience over time. By daring to differ, you invite your brand to stand out and shine with its unique persona. Your success lies in continually refining your persona based on feedback and changes in your audience or industry. In the end, a well-crafted brand persona elevates your image, proliferates your reach, and increases your influence, ultimately fostering a community of devoted followers and fans. Embark on this journey of difference, and experience the transition from ordinary to extraordinary!

Chapter 10. Navigating the Digital Landscape for Brand Amplification

In the digital age that defines our current epoch, your personal brand represents more than just a mere visual identifier; it conveys your fundamental essence, your purpose, your flag in the hyper-networked landscape. To successfully navigate through this webbed maze, understanding digital strategies to amplify your brand is vital.

10.1. Entrenched in Digital - Understanding Your Arena

Knowledge of platforms, their functionalities, audience demographics, and basic algorithms helps in deciding where to invest time and effort. Numerous platforms like LinkedIn, Instagram, Twitter, or personal blogs cater to different demographics. For example, if you are a business professional, LinkedIn may be your go-to platform. A graphic designer, on the other hand, can truly express their creativity on Instagram.

Remember, participation isn't limited to one platform. Feel free to engage on multiple fronts but consider the essence of your brand and pick platforms that make it shine. Create platform-specific content, understanding each channel's unique language.

Further, digital platforms are a double-edged sword. They amplify reach while subjecting you to noise. Planning your content and making full use of analytics can help you navigate this landscape more effectively.

10.2. An Orchestra of Content

Content is the linchpin in digital brand amplification. Reign supreme over the digital landscape without compromising your brand voice.

Know Your Voice: Establish your brand voice right at the outset. People should be able to recognize your content from across the virtual divide, just by your tone, style, or approach.

Educate, Entertain, Inspire: These are the three cornerstones of successful digital content. Create content that educates your audience, entertains them, or inspires them to act or think differently.

Dare to be Different: In the digital crowd, being different not just makes you stand but can also set new standards. Innovate with your content, the presentation style, the elements you use. The more unconventional, the better.

Consistency is King: Consistency not just in frequency but also in quality, tone, and messaging. Your audience should know what to expect. Surprise but never shock!

10.3. Crafting Cult Digital Presence - SEO & SEM Strategies

Using SEO (Search Engine Optimization) or SEM (Search Engine Marketing) strategies can significantly amplify your digital presence. Keywords are the foundations of SEO. They are the phrases that connect you to your audience. Use them effectively in your content, headers, titles, and meta descriptions.

Backlinks from credible sources give you credibility, boosting your digital reputation. SEM helps you boost your reach via targeted ads. Remember, these practices may take time and patience but they are long-term, invaluable investments.

10.4. Engage to Enlarge - Foster a Digital Community

Engagement isn't simply replying to comments but creating a community atmosphere where your audience feels involved. Involve your audience with innovative engagement tactics - live Q&A sessions, challenges, community forums, or even digital events. The primary goal is to make your audience feel connected, resonated with your brand.

10.5. Digital Listening and Responsiveness

In the era where everyone's opinion can be broadcasted globally in an instant, brands should consider social listening a staple. By monitoring mentions and responding to comments or criticisms, you show your audience that their opinion matters, while also gathering valuable insights.

Responsive brands win hearts. Manage criticisms gracefully, conceiving it as an opportunity to improve. A simple, truthful response can turn the tide favorably. In crisis situations, having a digital crisis management plan always prepares you to mitigate the situation swiftly.

10.6. Review, Revise, Reinvent

The digital landscape is dynamic. Keeping up with changes, constantly reviewing, and adapting your strategy is the key to your brand's longevity. Use analytics to understand what works, what doesn't, and what can be improved. Devise performance indicators such as engagement rates, reach, conversions, etc., and have regular checks.

Navigating the digital landscape may seem daunting initially, but, with strategic understanding and constant learning, it can undoubtedly lay down a broad highway for your brand's journey towards global recognition. Embrace digital, understand its quirks, speak its language, and you are on solid ground to create inspirational success stories.

Chapter 11. Sustainability and Authenticity: Maintaining Your Personal Brand for the Long Haul

An enduring, authentic personal brand upholds the test of times and the fickleness of trends. It isn't ephemeral; it grows, evolves, and delivers consistent value, cementing your indelible mark in your chosen industry. Thus, the journey of personal branding doesn't culminate once you've established your brand. Igniting vivacity and genuineness in your personal brand entails a perennial commitment—a commitment to sustainability and authenticity.

11.1. The Tenets of Authenticity

Authenticity is being true to your core values, beliefs, and ideas—exhibiting them unabashedly in every facet of your personal brand. An authentic personal brand doesn't resort to artifice or adopt any pretentious façade. Instead, it displays an altruistic representation of who you are.

1. **Transparency**: Be completely open and honest about your values, beliefs, opinions, and experiences that you bring forth.

2. **Consistency**: There should always be consistency between what you express and your actions. This paves the way for trust and credibility in your brand.

3. **Originality**: Embrace your uniqueness and let it surface throughout your personal brand communication.

11.2. Sustaining Your Brand: A Long-term Commitment

Maintaining a personal brand is predominantly about sustaining its initial vigour and enthusiasm. Your interactions must embody your personal brand tenets—making it visible in all your transactions. Moreover, as time progresses and as you continue to grow, laudably, accommodate for evolution within your personal brand.

1. **Reassessment and Reinvigoration**: Regularly evaluate your personal brand's relevance, and employ the necessary amendments to foster connection with your audience.

2. **Adaptation and Innovation**: As you evolve, so should your personal brand. Stay alert to market changes and adjust your personal brand accordingly.

3. **Advancement and Development**: Commit to personal growth and see it reflect in your brand. Sharpen your skills, acquire more knowledge, and let your personal brand be a testament to continuous development.

11.3. Mastering the Art of Criticism

Evolution of your personal brand isn't just about self-improvement but also welcoming corrective feedback with a poised and open mind. Societal criticism is part and parcel of your advancement, feeding your progress rather than impeding it. Here's how to navigate the ambiguous waters of criticism:

1. **Listen Actively**: Consciously listen to the critique rather than merely hearing it.

2. **Analyse Judiciously**: Assess if there's any truth to the comments. If yes, it's a chance for development. If no, let it slide without impacting your personal brand.

3. **Respond Graciously**: Always respond to criticism professionally and respectfully.

11.4. Setting Personal Brand Boundaries

In an era of rampant social media interactions, it's crucial to establish boundaries to protect your personal brand. From deciding how much to reveal about your personal life to maintaining cordial relationships online, setting boundaries is paramount to upkeeping an effective personal brand.

1. **Privacy Maintenance**: Decide upon what aspects of your life you are comfortable sharing publicly.

2. **Online Etiquette**: Always react and respond to every situation courteously and professionally.

3. **Strategic Involvement**: Cautiously participate in debates and discussions in line with your brand values.

Personal branding is a journey akin to self-discovery, a lifelong commitment to sustainability and authenticity. Witness your brand mold and flourish with you, making a distinct mark in your industry, establishing your voice as your ultimate branding ally. As you adapt, revise and refine, your brand will continue to resonate with many, showcasing your evolution as a consummate professional.

www.ingramcontent.com/pod-product-compliance
Lightning Source LLC
Chambersburg PA
CBHW060902260726

48661CB00008B/3402